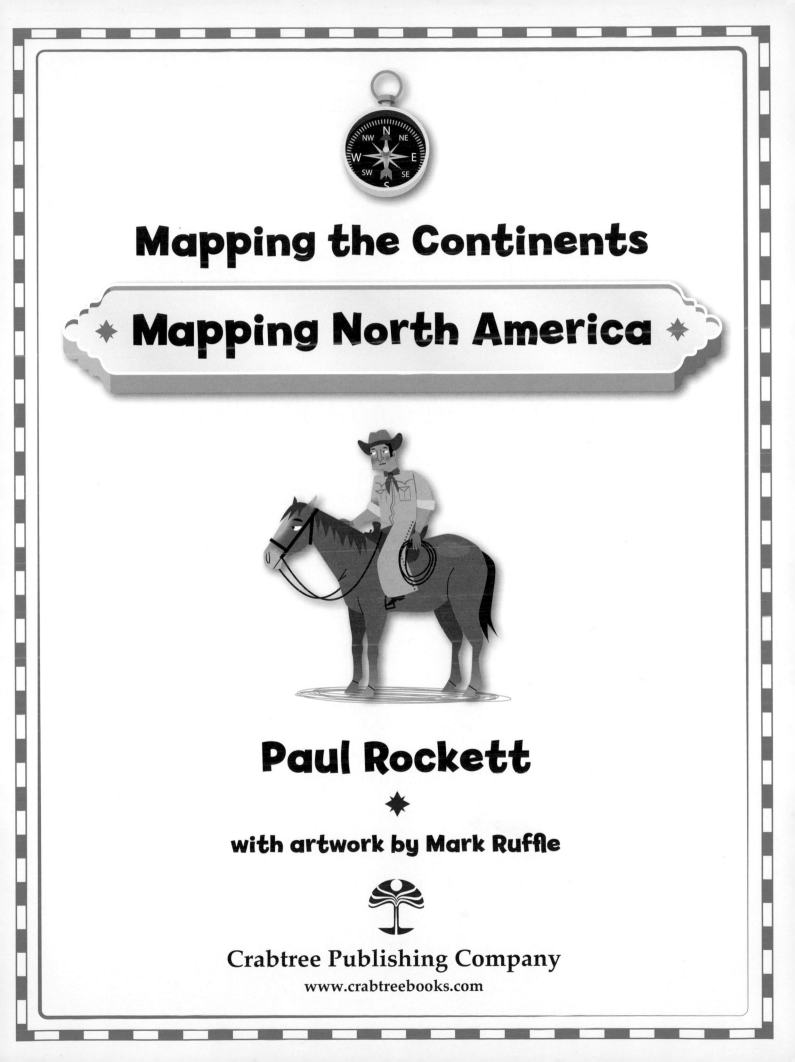

Mapping the Continents

Mapping North America

Paul Rockett

✦

with artwork by Mark Ruffle

Crabtree Publishing Company

www.crabtreebooks.com

Crabtree Publishing Company
www.crabtreebooks.com
1-800-387-7650

Published in Canada
616 Welland Ave.
St. Catharines, ON
L2M 5V6

Published in the United States
PMB 59051, 350 Fifth Ave.
59th Floor,
New York, NY

Published in 2017 by CRABTREE PUBLISHING COMPANY.

First published in 2015 by The Watts Publishing Group
(An imprint of Hachette Children's Group)
Copyright © The Watts Publishing Group 2015

Author: Paul Rockett

Editorial director: Kathy Middleton

Editors: Adrian Cole, and Ellen Rodger

Proofreader: Wendy Scavuzzo

Series design and illustration:
 Mark Ruffle, www.rufflebrothers.com

Prepress technician: Katherine Berti

Print and production coordinator: Katherine Berti

Printed in Canada/072016/PB20160525

Picture credits:
Aerial Archives.com/Alamy: 21t; All Canada Photos/Alamy: 15t; NASA, courtesy of Jacques Descloitres, MODIS Land Rapid Response Team at NASA GSFC: 13b; Photogenes: 8b; Wikimedia Commons: 6-7, 21b; Wollertz/Shutterstock: 17; Sergey Yechikov/Shutterstock: 29; Zuma Press/Alamy: 25.

Every attempt has been made to clear copyright. Should there by any inadvertent omission please apply to the publisher for rectification.

Library and Archives Canada Cataloguing in Publication

Rockett, Paul, author
 Mapping North America / Paul Rockett.

(Mapping the continents)
Includes index.
Issued in print and electronic formats.
ISBN 978-0-7787-2616-6 (hardback).--
ISBN 978-0-7787-2622-7 (paperback).--
ISBN 978-1-4271-1783-0 (html)

 1. North America--Juvenile literature. 2. Cartography--North America--Juvenile literature. 3. North America--Geography--Juvenile literature. 4. North America--Description and travel--Juvenile literature. 5. North America--Maps--Juvenile literature. I. Title.

E38.5.R64 2016   j917   C2016-902658-2
                                      C2016-902659-0

Library of Congress Cataloging-in-Publication Data

CIP available at the Library of Congress

Contents

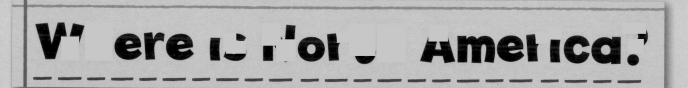

North America is the third-largest continent in the world, and covers about 4.8 percent of Earth's surface. It's a continent filled with a wide range of wildlife, cultures, and climates, stretching down from the Arctic chill of Greenland to the tropical heat of Costa Rica's Cocos Island.

North America

North American regions

North America is made up of countries that are sometimes split into smaller regions.

Canada

United States

United States and Canada

Some geographers consider North America to be just the United States and Canada.

Central America

The countries below the United States and above South America are sometimes grouped together as one region called Central America. This is because the shape of the land appears to be separate from the rest of North America, and the countries there share a similar culture and language.

South America

The Caribbean

The Caribbean refers to the Caribbean Sea and its chain of islands. Although the Caribbean is part of North America, it is not attached to the mainland of the continent.

Latin America

The countries of Central America, the Caribbean, and the continent of South America are sometimes grouped under the name Latin America. They were once part of empires ruled from southern Europe (see pages 8–9). As a result, most people in these countries speak the Latin-based languages of Spanish or Portuguese.

Supercontinent

North America was once part of a **supercontinent** called Laurasia. It broke apart into separate continents about 66 million to 30 million years ago.

Earth's surface is made up of **tectonic plates**, which are massive sections of rock that move slowly. This movement caused the supercontinent to break up into many smaller continents. North America sits on two tectonic plates—the North American Plate and the Caribbean Plate.

North America

Europe and Asia

South America

Africa

Antarctica

Laurasia

North American Plate

Caribbean Plate

South American Plate

Bering Land Bridge

Around 20,000 years ago, North America was connected to Asia by a stretch of land called the Bering Land Bridge. This land is now underwater. The first human inhabitants of North America are believed to have walked over the Bering Land Bridge from Asia.

Asia

Bering Land Bridge

North America

Present-day landmass

Landmass that existed 20,000 years ago

Possible migration route

Arctic Ocean

Pacific Ocean

North America

Atlantic Ocean

South America

Locating North America

We can describe the location of North America in relation to the areas of land and water that surround it, as well as using the points on a compass.

- North America is west of the Atlantic Ocean
- The Arctic Ocean is north of North America
- North America is north of South America
- North America is east of the Pacific Ocean

Countries

North America is made up of 23 countries, but also includes a number of islands that are still under the rule of European countries. North America's population has a diverse mix of backgrounds, descending from its **Indigenous peoples**, **colonial** settlers, African slaves, and later **immigrants** from Europe, Africa, the Middle East, and Asia.

Kingdom of Denmark

While Greenland is geographically part of North America, it is politically connected to Europe. It was a Danish colony and is still part of the Kingdom of Denmark.

Greenland
Greenland is the largest island in the world.

Canada

United States

Mexico

Dominican Republic

Bahamas

Cuba

Belize

Guatemala

Honduras

El Salvador

Nicaragua

Costa Rica

Panama

Barbados

1   Jamaica

2   Haiti

3   Saint Kitts and Nevis

4   Antigua and Barbuda

5   Dominica

6   Saint Lucia

7   Saint Vincent and the Grenadines

8   Grenada

9   Trinidad and Tobago

Colum us and for

The maps of North America that we use today were developed from maps made by European explorers during the 1400s and 1500s. Other types of maps made by Native peoples of North America recorded journeys over land and on lakes, rivers, and out to the open ocean.

Pre-Columbian cultures

The period of history before the arrival of Christopher Columbus (see opposite page) is called the pre-Columbian period. In pre-Columbian times, many different nations of Indigenous peoples lived in North America. They belonged to different cultures and spoke different languages.

These are some of the many pre-Columbian peoples that existed in North America. Many nations still exist today, and celebrate parts of their unique cultures and speak their language.

Inuit

Native peoples

Arawak

Aztecs and Mayans

Inuit wooden maps

Up until about 300 years ago, the Inuit who live along the coast of Greenland used wooden maps. These three-dimensional maps show the rugged coastline. They were carved from of a piece of wood, with bumps and notches representing **fjords**, islands, and glaciers.

First European settlements

It's thought that the first Europeans to arrive in North America were the Vikings. They sailed to Greenland around 982 C.E. and to Newfoundland, Canada, around 986 C.E.

Christopher Columbus

In 1492, Christopher Columbus, an explorer for Spain, set sail from Europe. He wanted to find a route west to Asia, but he didn't make it and instead landed in the Bahamas.

Between 1492 and 1504, Columbus made four separate voyages to North America. He explored the Caribbean islands and the coast of Central America—areas previously unknown to Europe.

First voyage, 1492–1493

Second voyage, 1493–1496

Fourth voyage, 1502–1504

Third voyage, 1498–1500

The use of wood meant that the maps survived harsh weather conditions, and the carved shapes allowed the user to understand the geography of the area by feeling the map as well as looking at it.

Aztec codices

The Aztecs were a group of people who, from around 1345 to 1521, built up a powerful **empire** in northern Mexico. Their civilization was wiped out by Spanish invaders (see page 20) and an outbreak of smallpox.

The Aztecs made codices—painted manuscripts made of one long sheet of paper folded up like an accordion. These featured pictures and symbols recorded important events, family information, and geographical landmarks.

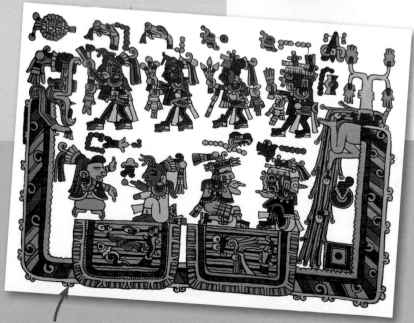

This image is copied from the Aztec manuscript Codex Zouche-Nuttall. *The symbols of waterfalls and caves helped historians to find the actual location shown.*

Independent states

After the voyages of Columbus, large areas of North America were claimed and colonized by the European countries of Spain, France, and Great Britain. These colonial powers, and independent rule for the colonies later on, all shaped the borders we recognize today.

- land claimed by Great Britain
- land claimed by France
- land claimed by Spain
- unorganized territory

European territory in North America, 1713

Independence

North American independence from European powers began in the 1700s. This changed the shape of many of North America's countries, with borders being redrawn across the continent.

United States of America

On July 4, 1776, 13 British colonies declared independence from Great Britain, and the United States of America was formed. More states joined the union over the next 183 years, with Hawaii joining last in 1959. Interestingly, Hawaii is not part of the North American continent—or any continent.

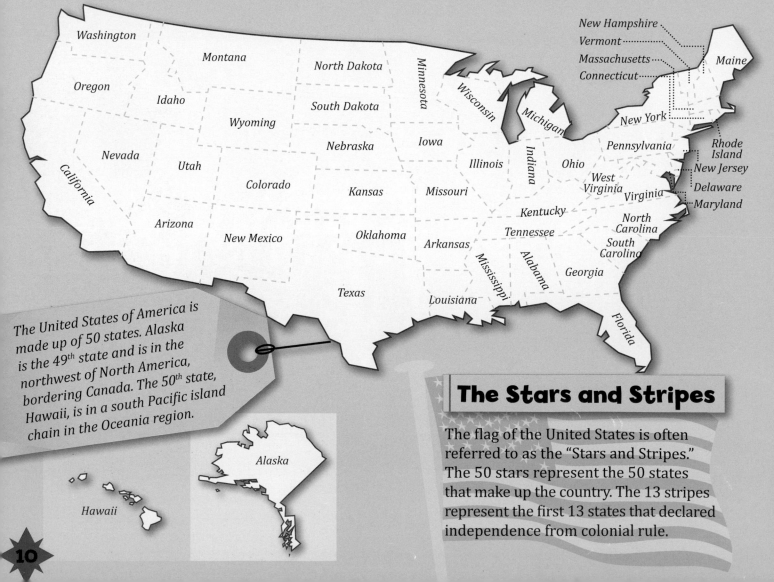

The United States of America is made up of 50 states. Alaska is the 49th state and is in the northwest of North America, bordering Canada. The 50th state, Hawaii, is in a south Pacific island chain in the Oceania region.

The Stars and Stripes

The flag of the United States is often referred to as the "Stars and Stripes." The 50 stars represent the 50 states that make up the country. The 13 stripes represent the first 13 states that declared independence from colonial rule.

Canada

At the end of the Seven Years' War in 1763, France lost its Canadian territory to Great Britain. On July 1, 1867, the remaining British colonies joined together to form the Dominion of Canada. July 1 was called Dominion Day, but is now celebrated as Canada Day.

Yukon

Northwest Territories

Nunavut

British Columbia

Alberta

Saskatchewan

Manitoba

Ontario

Quebec

Newfoundland and Labrador

Prince Edward Island

Nova Scotia

New Brunswick

Canada is made up of 10 provinces and 3 territories, shown above.

This map shows the territories that were ruled under the first Mexican Empire.

Central America

Spain's colonies gained independence in 1821, with Mexico forming the First Mexican Empire, and the provinces of Central America forming the Republic of Central America. By 1840, the Republic broke up into separate countries. At the same time, the Mexican American War (1846–1848) led to Mexico losing half of its northern territory to the United States.

The Caribbean

Some of the Caribbean islands remain colonies or regions of European countries or the United States, such as the Dutch island, Aruba. Others have gained their independence, beginning with Haiti in 1804, up to Saint Kitts and Nevis in 1983.

Climates

North America is positioned between two imaginary lines running horizontally across the continent in the north and south. These are the Arctic Circle and the Tropic of Cancer. They are areas of extreme climate, with dry to **subarctic** climates existing in between.

Coldest climate

Greenland has the coldest climate in North America, with 80 percent of its mainland covered in a frozen **glacier** ice sheet all year round. The average daily temperature in its capital city, Nuuk, ranges from 18 °F to 45 °F (-8 °C to 7 °C).

Tropic of Cancer

The Tropic of Cancer marks out a stretch of land north of the equator. The line runs through Mexico and the Bahamas, with the area between that line and the **equator** known as the tropics. The weather is always warm there, with **dry** and **humid subtropical climates.**

Tropic of Cancer

Arctic Circle

The **climate** within the Arctic Circle is very cold and much of the area is always covered with ice. The **polar** climate passes through Greenland, Canada, and Alaska.

Greenland

Appalachian Mountains

Tornado alley

Rocky Mountains

66
22
45
51
45
39
37
57
96
62
155
53
11
5
2
3
11

Climate zones:

- tropical
- dry
- humid subtropical
- Mediterranean
- subarctic
- polar

Highest average number of tornadoes a year

X

Hurricanes

Hurricanes are rotating systems of clouds and thunderstorms that form over **tropical** water. In North America, they occur in areas that are in the Tropic of Cancer, where the water is warm. Sometimes hurricanes travel inland, causing death, destruction to buildings, and damage to wildlife habitats.

Tropic of Cancer

The hurricane season here is from June to November.

The hurricane season here is from May to October.

Hurricane Scale

Scale	Damage
1	Minimal
2	Moderate
3	Extensive
4	Extreme
5	Catastrophic

Hurricane Ivan

In 2004, Hurricane Ivan traveled from the west coast of Africa toward the Caribbean and the United States. It was an incredibly destructive hurricane, causing billions of dollars in damage. It was also responsible for 121 deaths. As it traveled, its speed and strength changed. A hurricane scale represents the changing stages.

North American route of Hurricane Ivan

A satellite image of Hurricane Ivan off the coast of Cuba, 2004

Tornado Alley

Tornado Alley is the name given to an area that has a lot of tornado activity. In the United States, this covers an area of land in the mid- and south-central states, sheltered by the Rocky Mountains and the Appalachian Mountains. In the summer, this dry climate gets very hot, with air from the ground rising and spinning upward in a funnel where it meets cooler air above.

Wildlife

The wildlife of North America ranges from the big and furry to the small and scaly. The harsh habitats of the Arctic, the heat of the south, and the changing seasons lead many creatures to **migrate** across the continent.

Caribou

The caribou is a member of the deer family, and is the only deer species in which males and females both have antlers. They live in Alaska and in Canada. During the summer, large herds of caribou migrate far north to calving grounds where the females give birth.

Peary caribou

Barren-ground caribou

North American beaver

Woodland caribou

American bison

The tallest living tree in the world can be found growing in the Redwood National Park in California. It's a coast redwood, measuring 380 feet (116 m) in height.

Bald eagle

Jaguar

Reef gecko

14

Monarch butterfly

Monarch butterflies migrate from the northeast of North America down to Mexico each winter, traveling up to 3,000 miles (4,828 km). There, they hibernate over winter in a warmer climate. This arrow shows the migration route of the monarch butterflies.

Everglades

The Florida Everglades is one of the largest **wetlands** in the world. The landscape is made up of different habitats. Each habitat has many ecosystems, where a community of animals and plants interact with each other as a source of food and shelter.

Habitats of the Everglades:

- sawgrass marshes
- freshwater **slough**
- mangrove swamps
- pinelands
- hardwood **hammocks**

An Everglades food chain:

The American alligator lives in the Everglades. It sits at the top of a **food chain**, feeding off other animals in the swamps, marshlands, and the edges of the hammocks.

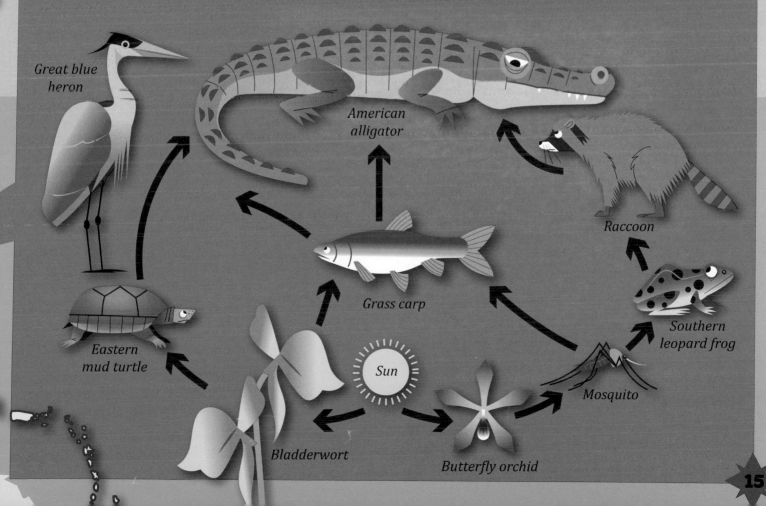

Great blue heron

American alligator

Raccoon

Grass carp

Southern leopard frog

Eastern mud turtle

Sun

Mosquito

Bladderwort

Butterfly orchid

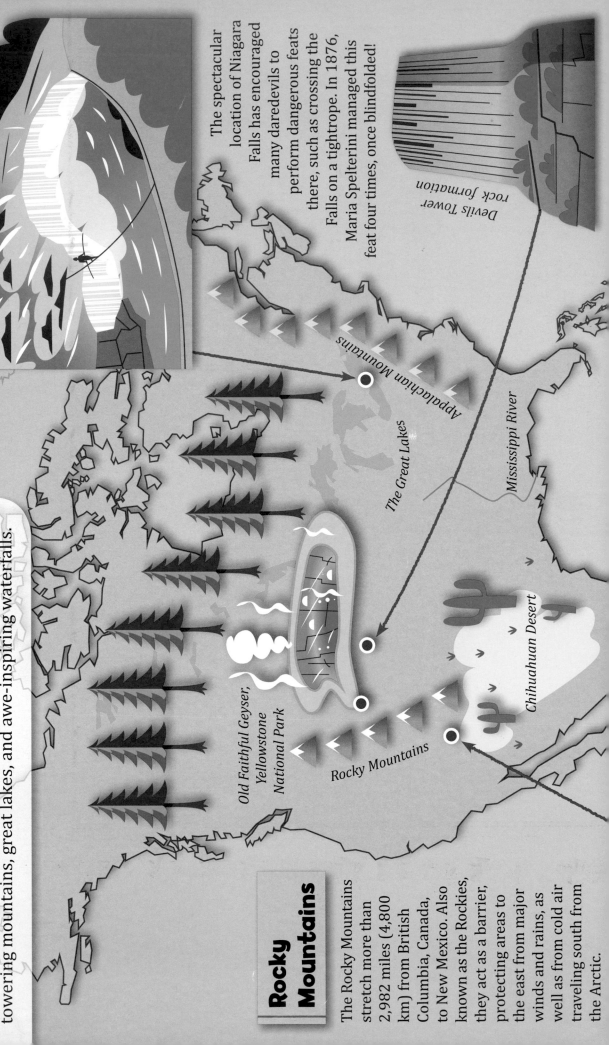

Natural landmarks

The North American landscape ranges from vast open plains to thick forests and dry deserts. It's also home to giant canyons, towering mountains, great lakes, and awe-inspiring waterfalls.

Niagara Falls

Niagara Falls is on the border between Canada and the United States. It's made up of three waterfalls—the Horseshoe Falls, the American Falls, and the Bridal Veil Falls. The Horseshoe Falls is the largest, with a vertical drop of 187 feet (57 m).

The spectacular location of Niagara Falls has encouraged many daredevils to perform dangerous feats there, such as crossing the Falls on a tightrope. In 1876, Maria Spelterini managed this feat four times, once blindfolded!

Devils Tower rock formation

Appalachian Mountains

The Great Lakes

Mississippi River

Old Faithful Geyser, Yellowstone National Park

Chihuahuan Desert

Rocky Mountains

Rocky Mountains

The Rocky Mountains stretch more than 2,982 miles (4,800 km) from British Columbia, Canada, to New Mexico. Also known as the Rockies, they act as a barrier, protecting areas to the east from major winds and rains, as well as from cold air traveling south from the Arctic.

Great Blue Hole

An aerial view of the coast surrounding Belize reveals a deep blue circle in the ocean. This is known as the Great Blue Hole. It measures 984 feet (300 m) across and is 407 feet (124 m) deep.

It was formed from a system of limestone caves under the ocean bed that collapsed and left a deep hole. It's believed to be the largest hole of its kind and is a popular site for scuba divers to explore tropical marine life.

The Grand Canyon

Around five million tourists visit the Grand Canyon each year. It's 269 miles (433 km) long, stretches 10 miles (16 km) across and is around 1 mile (1.6 km) deep. The canyon has been carved out by the Colorado River that runs through it.

Popocatépetl

Popocatépetl in Mexico is a stunning snow-capped volcano whose name means "smoking mountain" in Aztec. It is one of the world's most active volcanoes. A future major eruption would threaten the lives of the 20 million people who live nearby in Mexico City.

uman-made lanjmarks

From the ancient pyramids hidden in the forests of Central America to the modern architectural feats towering in the United States, the landscape of North America is covered with human-made landmarks that show great ambition.

Mount Rushmore National Memorial

Between 1927 and 1941, the giant heads of four American presidents were sculpted into the side of Mount Rushmore in South Dakota. The monument is 59 feet (18 m) high, with each head the height of a six-story building and each nose around 19 feet (6 m) long.

George Washington
(1732–1799)

Thomas Jefferson
(1743–1826)

Theodore Roosevelt
(1858–1919)

Abraham Lincoln
(1809–1865)

Golden Gate Bridge

Painted a striking orange color, the Golden Gate Bridge opened in 1937. At the time, it was the longest suspension bridge in the world. With a total length of 8,980 feet (2,737 m), it spans the Golden Gate Strait in California, connecting San Francisco with Marin County.

The White House, Washington, DC

First Nations totem pole, Vancouver Island

The Pentagon, Arlington County

Disneyland castle, Florida

Stone heads (Olmec)

*Inukshuk,
Baffin Island*

*Empire State Building,
New York City*

Statue of Liberty

The Statue of Liberty represents the Roman goddess of freedom. It was a gift from France, presented in 1886 to celebrate American independence and the abolition of slavery. It stands at 305 feet (93 m) in height from the ground to the torch, welcoming boats as they pass by into New York Harbor.

El Castillo

El Castillo, also known as the Temple of Kukulcán, is a step pyramid that is central to the ancient Mayan city of Chichen Itza.

The pyramid is more than 1,500 years old, and was designed to reflect the Mayan calendar. There are 91 steps on all four sides, and with a temple platform at the top, there are a total of 365 steps, which is the number of days in a year.

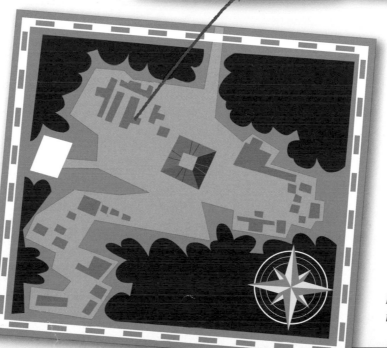

*Map of Chichen Itza,
in Yucatán, Mexico*

Settlements

This map shows the population density of North America. The most populated areas are major cities, and the places with the least number of people are areas of vast wilderness, such as the Arctic tundra or deserts.

People per sq km:

1
10
25
50
100
101+

Whapmagoostui and Kuujjuarapik

New York City

Mexico City

St. George's

Mexico City

Mexico City is one of the most crowded cities in the world. It's home to 20 percent of Mexico's population—around nine million people. It's been estimated that the population will reach 23 million by 2020.

The city used to be swampland, where the Aztecs built the city of Tenochtitlan more than 600 years ago. When the Spanish arrived in the 1500s, the Aztec city was destroyed and built over.

New York City

New York City is the most populous city in the United States. It is made up of five boroughs:

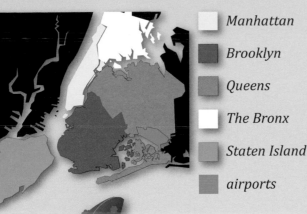

- Manhattan
- Brooklyn
- Queens
- The Bronx
- Staten Island
- airports

The central streets of Manhattan were built following a simple grid, with blocks laid out in orderly rows. This helped safeguard against overcrowding, fire, and disease—all things that are harder to contain in cities with a jumbled street plan.

Whapmagoostui and Kuujjuarapik

In the northwest of Quebec are two villages inhabited by two different Indigenous communities.

Whapmagoostui is home to the Cree, a group of Native peoples. Less than 1.9 miles (3 km) away is Kuujjuarapik, where an Inuit community lives. Both communities made permanent settlements there more than 70 years ago, when it was a center for whale hunting.

Kuujjuarapik

Whapmagoostui

Great Whale River

The Cree and the Inuit were traditionally nomadic peoples, who moved around building temporary homes in areas where they fished and hunted.

The Cree built ridge pole lodges that were portable and easy to construct.

When hunting in the winter, the Inuit built temporary snowhouses, known as igloos. These were made out of blocks of tightly packed snow and could be built in around 20 to 30 minutes.

St George's

The houses in St George's, the capital of Grenada, are designed to cope with the weather and landscape.

The roofs have ridges on them, so that the rain trickles down into water tanks.

The houses are painted white to help reflect the heat of the Sun.

There is very little flat land in St George's, so many houses are built on stilts.

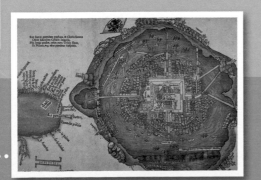

This map, drawn by Spanish conquerers in 1524, shows the layout of Tenochtitlan.

Industries

The North American economy varies from country to country, and region to region. A resource-based economy is dominant in Canada's north, while high-tech industries are prominent in California. Farming is the main business in many Central American countries, and tourism is a big money-maker in the Caribbean islands.

Main industries in North America

Crops:
- Bananas
- Corn
- Sugar cane
- Coffee
- Wheat
- Vineyards
- Tobacco

Industries:
- Automobiles
- Forestry
- High tech
- Textiles
- Fishing
- Tourism
- Mining
- Oil

Livestock:
- Cattle
- Sheep
- Pigs

Silicon Valley

Pennsylvania

The Caribbean

Atlantic Ocean

Pacific Ocean

Panama Canal

The Panama Canal is a 48 mile (77.1 km) human-made channel that connects the Atlantic Ocean with the Pacific Ocean. Before the canal, trade ships had to sail down and around the southernmost tip of South America to get from one side of North America to the other.

Rust Belt

The northwest United States used to be called "the industrial heartland." This area is rich in coal and iron, and housed large factories for the production of steel, cars, and weapons. In the 1980s, competition from overseas led to a decline in these industries. Many people moved away to find work elsewhere and the factories were left to rust. This led the area to be known as the rust belt.

An abandoned steel factory in Pennsylvania

The United States still has one of the largest manufacturing economies in the world. It leads the world in making airplanes and still has a strong market for American-made cars, produced by companies such as Ford and General Motors.

Silicon Valley

Silicon Valley is the name given to an area in California that is home to many of the world's largest technology corporations, including Apple, Facebook, and Google.

The "silicon" in its name refers to a fine sand-like material used in the making of computer chips—an essential part of products that have been made in Silicon Valley.

12,986 miles
(20,900 km)

New York

San Francisco

5,200 miles
(8,370 km)

More than 1,000 heavily loaded ships sail through the Panama Canal each month, with the canal generating around $2.6 billion a year for Panama.

Farming

Farming is big business for all of the countries in North America. Helped by the tropical climate, farming is the largest industry in Central America and the Caribbean. Top crops include tobacco, bananas, sugar cane, coffee, cocoa beans, and coconuts.

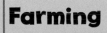

Sports

Sports are very popular in North America. Some of the greatest legends of sports live and play in North America. And many major sporting events are held throughout the continent each year.

Sporting profiles:

Billie Jean King is an American tennis legend. She won 39 major titles and ranked number one in the world five times between 1966 and 1972. King was a pioneer for women in sports, pushing for equal treatment and prize money.

Billie Jean King

Sporting profiles:

Nicknamed "Lightning Bolt," Jamaican athlete Usain Bolt is the fastest sprinter in the world. In 2009, he set a new world record for the 100 m, with a time of 9.58 seconds, and in the 200 m, with a time of 19.19 seconds.

Usain Bolt

Ice hockey

Hockey evolved from ancient ball-and-stick games. Ice hockey games were played on frozen rivers and ponds in Nova Scotia, Canada, in the early 1800s. The National Hockey League (NHL) began in Montreal with four Canadian teams in 1917. There are now 30 teams throughout Canada and the United States.

Cricket

Cricket is the most popular sport in the Caribbean. It was introduced by the British army in the early 1800s. One of the top teams in the world is the West Indies cricket team, also known as the "Windies." The team represents 15 Caribbean countries.

Women's soccer

Women's soccer is increasing in popularity around the world, with the United States leading the way. The American national team is one of the most successful in the world, and has won the FIFA Women's World Cup three times.

Mexican wrestling

In Mexico, professional wrestling is known as *lucha libre*. Mexican wrestling features acrobatic flying moves and the wrestlers wear colorful masks that are decorated to represent animals, gods, and ancient heroes.

Culture

North America celebrates its history in festivals, storytelling, and the arts. While much of North American culture has a local identity, its influence is felt all over the world. You only need to turn on the TV, the radio, or go to the movies, to see or feel the effect of North American folk and popular culture.

Hollywood

Hollywood is a district in Los Angeles that is the center of the American film industry. Many big film production studios have been based there since the 1920s, producing blockbuster movies that are hugely successful all around the world.

The Wild West

Mississippi River

HOLLYWOOD

The Wild West refers to an area of land and a time during the 1800s, when European settlers moved west of the Mississippi River. In the United States, they traveled across large open plains using horse- and ox-drawn wagons. In Canada, the newly-built Canadian Pacific Railway brought settlers to the prairies and west coast in the late 1800s.

There was great conflict between the settlers and Native tribes over land. Many battles were fought, which forever altered the Native way of life.

Cowboy and Wild West stories have inspired many Hollywood movies.

Hip-hop

Hip-hop culture includes DJing, rapping, breakdancing, and graffiti art. It grew out of 1970s New York, with young African Americans throwing block parties, sampling and scratching records, and rapping over them. Now popular all over the world, hip-hop culture often addresses issues of race and class.

The skull is the symbol of the Day of the Dead. Some skulls are worn as masks, while others, made of chocolate or sugar, are eaten.

Day of the Dead

The Day of the Dead is a Mexican holiday in which people get together to remember those that have died. Rather than being a sad occasion, it is a time of joyous celebration with parades and street parties. The dead are honored with gifts, and their gravestones are decorated with flowers.

Religion

Christianity is the largest, but not the only, religion practiced in North America. In Latin American countries and Canada, the majority of Christians are Catholic, whereas the majority in the United States are Protestant. Christianity was brought to North America by European colonizers.

One of the largest Roman Catholic churches in the world is the Basilica of Our Lady of Guadalupe, in Mexico City.

Food and drink

North America is so geographically and culturally diverse that there isn't just one cuisine. The United States is known as the home of the hamburger, but potato chips, buffalo chicken wings, and chicken fried steak were also invented there. Corn, or maize, is a major crop throughout North America. Corn flour foods such as tortillas, tamales, tacos, and pupusas are staples throughout Mexico and Central America. These foods and other tasty North America treats are now popular around the world.

Muktuk

Muktuk is an Inuit dish of frozen whale skin and **blubber**. Taken from hunted narwhal, beluga, or bowhead whales, the skin is rubbery and hazelnut-flavored, while the blubber is chewy.

Fast food

Fast food is food that is prepared quickly, such as hamburgers, pizzas, or fried chicken, and bought cheaply in restaurants. It first became popular in the 1950s, in the United States. The world's biggest fast-food chains, including McDonald's, KFC, and Burger King, all started out in the United States.

Apple pie

Lobster

Maple syrup

Butter tart

Thanksgiving turkey

Creole chicken is a traditional Haitian dish. The chicken is marinated in garlic, lime, and green peppers, and cooked in oil with hot red peppers, tomatoes, and onion.

Chicago-style deep dish pizza

Fried yojoa fish

Pupusa

Guacamole with tortilla chips

Creole cuisine

Creole cuisine is hot and peppery, coming from the multicultural **heritage** of French, Spanish, African, and Caribbean foods and flavors. Both Haiti and the state of Louisiana have a history of Creole culture that is reflected in their food.

Jambalaya is a popular Creole dish in Louisiana. Its ingredients include spicy sausage, peppers, onion, garlic, rice, shrimp, tomatoes, paprika, and cayenne pepper.

Tamale

The tamale dates back to the Mayan civilization in Mexico, and is today widely eaten in all Central American countries. It's made from chopped meat and crushed peppers, packed in a parcel made from corn flour dough, wrapped in husks or leaves, then steamed.

Further information

COUNTRY	POPULATION	SIZE SQ MI*	CAPITAL CITY	MAIN LANGUAGES
United States	325,127,634	3,794,098.9	Washington, DC	English
Mexico	125,235,587	758,449.1	Mexico City	Spanish
Canada	35,871,283	3,855,101.1	Ottawa	English, French
Guatemala	16,255,094	42,042.3	Guatemala City	Spanish
Cuba	11,248,783	42,803.3	Havana	Spanish
Dominican Republic	10,652,136	18,791.6	Santo Domingo	Spanish
Haiti	10,603,731	10,714.3	Port-au-Prince	French, Haitian Creole
Honduras	8,423,917	43,278.2	Tegucigalpa	Spanish
El Salvador	6,426,002	8,124	San Salvador	Spanish
Nicaragua	6,256,510	50,336.1	Managua	Spanish
Costa Rica	5,001,657	19,729.8	San José	Spanish
Panama	3,987,866	29,119.8	Panama City	Spanish
Jamaica	2,813,276	4,243.6	Kingston	English
Trinidad and Tobago	1,346,697	1,979.9	Port of Spain	English
Martinique	405,688	435.5	Fort-de-France	French
Bahamas	387,598	5,359.1	Nassau	English
Puerto Rico	368,058	3,515	San Juan	Spanish
Belize	347,598	8,867.2	Belmopan	English, Spanish
Barbados	287,482	166.2	Bridgetown	English
Saint Lucia	184,937	237.8	Castries	English
Saint Vincent and the Grenadines	109,374	150.2	Kingstown	English
Grenada	106,694	132.8	St George's	Dutch, Papiamento
Antigua and Barbuda	91,822	170.9	St John's	English
Dominica	72,680	290	Roseau	English
Greenland	57,275	836,330.1	Nuuk	Greenlandic, Danish
Saint Kitts and Nevis	55,372	100.8	Basseterre	English
St. Pierre and Miquelon	6,049	93.4	Saint-Pierre	French

*To arrive at square kilometers (sq km), divide a number in square miles (sq mi) by 0.386102.

Glossary

blubber
a layer of fat found between the skin and muscle of a whale

climate
average weather conditions in a particular area

colonial
relating to the colonies, which are countries or areas controlled by another country and occupied by settlers from that country

dry (climate)
a climate zone that receives little rainfall with land that can be too dry to support much vegetation; experienced in areas such as deserts and grasslands

empire
a group of countries governed under a single authority, such as under one ruler or country

equator
an imaginary line drawn around Earth separating the northern and southern hemispheres

fjord
a long narrow inlet of water between steep walls of rock

food chain
a series of living things or organisms; each is dependent on the next organism lower down the chain as a source of food

glacier
a mass of ice that moves very slowly over a large area of land

hammocks
an elevated area of fertile land, usually with hardwood trees and surrounded by wetlands

heritage
items of historical importance for a country, such as buildings and past traditions

humid subtropical climate
a climate zone characterized by hot, humid summers and mild to cool winters

immigrants
people who come to live permanently in a foreign country

Indigenous peoples
communities living in a particular country or region that have lived there long before the invasion and settlement of a foreign society, such as the Native peoples in the United States and Canada

migrate
seasonal movement of animals from one region to another

polar
describing climate zones found surrounding the North and South Poles, which are extremely cold and dry

slough
an area of marshy river with slow-moving water

subarctic
a climate zone that is found in areas south of the Arctic Circle, experiencing long, cold winters and short, cool to mild summers

supercontinent
a former large continent made up of several present-day continents that later broke off and drifted away

tectonic plates
plates under Earth's surface or crust that move and sometimes meet, causing earthquakes

tropical
a climate zone with hot, humid weather and high temperatures throughout the year

wetlands
areas of land covered in shallow water, such as swamps or marshes

Index